MANIPULATION

The Complete Psychologist's Guide to Highly Effective
Manipulation and Deception Techniques – Influence
People with NLP, Mind Control and Persuasion

Table of Contents

INTRODUCTION

While our lives might look all great and beautiful on the outside with an ideal upbringing, great education and a stellar career, we've all been victims of unsavory tactics used by people to have their way by preying on our feelings, self-worth and emotions.

We've all been part of manipulative relationships where the strings of our feelings and emotions were cleverly controlled by another person to fulfill their needs.

While humans at large thrive on love, kindness and gratitude, it cannot be denied that it can be a self-centered species at times. Yes, we can be self-serving by nature! You may not think being selfish or self-serving is a negative trait. Why shouldn't we think about ourselves? However, some folks take this self-centeredness too far. In their bid to serve their needs, they tread upon the feelings and emotions of others.

When people start resorting to intentional, calculated and cunning techniques for having their way, this is what makes it harmful and immoral. The intensity of this may vary from person to person depending on their upbringing, environment, personality, experiences, education and several other factors.

We all are guilty of using manipulation at some point, often without realizing it. In the same vein, we are often manipulated by people close to us without realizing that we are being victims of manipulation. And this is precisely what makes it so sinister and insidious. We are made to think, feel and act in a specific way to fulfill another person's need without consideration for our emotions.

For instance, you may be made to feel guilty about working hard or putting in long hours of work even though you are doing it to build a future for your loved ones. Or you'll be made to feel like you are an irresponsible person for taking a break from housework and letting yourself have fun with friends.

The stark reality about manipulation is that it originates from people who are grappling with issues related to security, self-confidence and comfort. They attempt to push their luck in a bid to hold other people down for fear of losing them. Manipulators operate from a deep sense of insecurity. Ironically, what they don't realize is that, in their bid to hold people down owing to the fear of losing them, they end up doing just that - losing people!

Other times, manipulators are simply out to take advantage of people to serve their cut throat, selfish purposes. They are cold, calculating and ruthless in their acts. There is no regard for the feelings and emotions of their victims. It is a 'dog-eat-dog' world according to them, and to survive, they believe they have to use other people.

Manipulators operate with a point of view that they must reach their end through whatever means it takes, and if it ends up hurting a few people along the way, so be it. These are people you should actively watch out for and avoid.

The purpose of this book is to make you aware of the sneaky tricks people use for manipulating others. It aims to uncover how people use emotional manipulation, mind control and persuasion to fulfill their own needs.

When you are able to identify clever manipulative techniques, it becomes easier to guard against them. You'll learn to read warning signs of manipulation and use practical techniques to safeguard your emotions and self-confidence, thus accomplishing complete immunity against people's sly tactics.

CHAPTER ONE

EXAMINING EMOTIONAL MANIPULATION

Have you lost count of the number of times you've been told, that if you love someone, you will or won't do something for them? Why do people equate an emotion like love with such frivolous matters as grabbing dinner at a particular restaurant or catching a new release movie? Well, that is the power of emotions. Emotions are a double-edged sword that can be leveraged both positively and negatively by people for fulfilling their needs.

During the 20th century, one of the planet's most powerful leaders recognized the power of emotions on people. He devoted years to getting the finer nuances of body language right by analyzing visuals of his posture, expressions, hand gestures and more. He mastered the art of spellbinding, almost hypnotizing, people through his public speeches and gestures. His name: Adolf Hitler.

The last thing you want is to be emotionally manipulated by everyone from your friends to co-workers to politicians to your partner. People using manipulation may knowingly or unknowingly disregard ethics and prey on your emotions to serve their needs.

While each of us is guilty of using manipulation (knowingly or unknowingly) at some point, what makes emotional manipulators different is they habitually trample upon people's emotions and feelings to serve their own selfish needs. It is a way of life for some people to use other people's feelings in a bid to increase their psychological hold or superiority over the person.

Manipulation is starkly different from persuasion. While persuasion awards the other person a right to select his/her response to a particular situation, manipulation does not give the victim the right to choose. Manipulation has only one way – the way your manipulator wants you to take. There is only one single 'correct choice': the manipulator's choice. There is zero regard or concern for your wishes, desires, choices and emotions. You will pay with hell if you don't pick the choice they want you to.

Typical manipulative tactics include:

- Complaining
- Playing victim
- Inducing guilt
- Comparing
- Offering excuses and rationalizing

- Feigning ignorance
- Emotional blackmail
- Evasiveness
- Demonstrating fake concern
- Undermining people
- Blaming others and using "Who me?" defenses
- Lying
- Denying
- False flattery
- Intimidation
- Giving the illusion of selflessness
- Shaming

Using foot in the door techniques

Here are different ways through which we experience emotional manipulation in our lives (and you may not have even been aware you were being manipulated):

1. Emotional manipulators play on people's fears. Emotional manipulators tend to blow facts out of proportion and highlight only specific points in a bid to instill fear in you. For example, a man who doesn't want his wife to pursue a full-time career outside the house may tell her something like, "Research reveals 60 percent of all divorces happen when both partners are engaged in full-time careers," sneakily hiding the fact that there can be reasons other than the woman's career or job.

This is cleverly constructed to prey on the woman's fear of losing the relationship as she gives in to her ambitions.

2. The actions and words of emotional manipulators seldom match. Emotional manipulators tell you exactly what they think you want to hear but will rarely follow it up with action. They will pledge commitment and support. However, when it comes to acting upon their commitment, they will make you feel guilty for coming up with unreasonable demands.

    At one point, they'll tell you how fortunate they are to know a person like you, and the next they'll be slamming you for being a burden. This is a clever tactic for undermining your own belief about your sanity. Emotional manipulators will keep saying things that suit their purpose and suddenly mold a perception to the contrary by doing the opposite of what they said to misbalance your sanity.

    Their help also comes at a price, which they'll sneakily claim in the future. They will constantly remind you of how they helped you and use that as a leverage to get you to feel obliged to them. If you are perpetually being reminded of a favor they willingly did for you, which makes you feel you owe them something, there are high chances you are being emotionally manipulated.

3. They are masters at distributing guilt. Few people leverage the power of guilt like practiced manipulators. Emotional manipulators induce guilt in other people to serve their needs. If you bring up an issue for discussion that's been bothering you,

they'll make you feel guilty about feeling the way you do, however justified your feelings are. Emotional manipulators will make you feel guilty for mentioning the issue. When you don't mention the issue, they'll make you feel miserable for not being open and talking about it.

All they do is keep stewing guilt in you, irrespective of the direction of your thoughts and actions. One way or another, they'll find reasons to make you feel guilty. When you are with an emotional manipulator, anything you choose to do is wrong. Irrespective of the problems you may be having collectively, an emotional manipulator will always make you feel it is only your fault. They will blame you for everything unfortunate happening in their life and build a strong sense of guilt within you.

4. They'll don the victim's role. Where emotional manipulation is concerned, nothing that happens is ever their mistake. Irrespective of their actions, they will always blame someone else for their failings.

They'll often harp on how they were made to do something by you. If you get angry or hurt, you are the one responsible for building unreasonable expectations. If they get angry or upset, you are responsible for hurting them. There is zero accountability for any action.

For example, if a person forgets their partner's birthday, and the partner gets upset about it, they'll generally apologize and promise to make good for it in future. However, an emotionally manipulative person will not just deny it is their fault; they will also make their partner feel miserable for blaming them.

They will go off about how stressed they've been of late, owing it to something the partner has done, that it's just impossible for them to remember it. The manipulator will go a step ahead and remind you of instances where you've forgotten something important to justify their fault.

5. Emotional manipulators expect too much, way too soon. From an interpersonal relationship to a business association, emotional manipulators are always moving in very fast, while overlooking a few steps along the way. They may share too much too early in a relationship and expect the other person to do the same.

Their vulnerability, transparency and sensitivity are a clever ruse. This is a 'special' charade to make you feel a part of their inner circle. Slowly and insidiously, you'll not just feel sorry about their feelings but also responsible for them.

6. Emotional manipulators belittle your faith in understanding reality. These people, you must hand it to them, are exceptionally skilled liars and cheats. They will confidently insist something happened when it didn't and deny it happened when it did. They do this in such a devious and underhanded manner that you begin questioning your own sanity.

For example, if you suspect your partner of having an affair and confront them about it, the emotionally manipulative partner will outright deny it (even though it is the truth), and in turn make you feel like an insane, suspicious person who doesn't have a grip on reality.

Even though your suspicion is not unfounded, you'll be made to feel guilty about spying around and not trusting your partner. It'll come to a point where you will begin questioning your own suspicious nature and sanity. I am sure many of you are nodding your head in agreement to this!

I know by now you've already identified such people and relationships. I have, and imagine, we weren't even aware of these snarky, insidious tactics when we were being manipulated.

7. Everyone must feel the way they do. Wow, this is another sneaky emotional manipulation technique used to suck other people into their emotional state. The emotional manipulator wants everyone to feel the way they are feeling. If they are in a foul mood, everyone around should be aware of it.

However, it doesn't end there. Not only should everyone know how they are feeling, they should also be sucked into the emotional state of the manipulator. Whatever other people are feeling or experiencing should be dropped , and they should instantly match the emotional frequency of the manipulator. This makes people around them feel like they are responsible for the emotional manipulator's feelings, and they alone should fix it.

8. Eagerness to help becomes a burden later. Emotional manipulators will volunteer to help initially (and pretty eagerly at that) only to make themselves look like martyrs later. They will act like what they initially agreed to do is a huge burden.

    If you remind them that they committed to the task, they'll turn around and make you feel like a paranoid person despite them appearing eager to help. The objective? To induce a feeling of guilt, feeling obliged towards them and probably even questioning your sanity!

9. One-upmanship games. Irrespective of the intensity of your problems and challenges, the manipulator will always make it come across as their problems are much worse. They will attempt to undermine the authenticity of your problems by constantly reinforcing how much bigger their problems or challenges are.

    They'll make you feel guilty for complaining about 'trivial' things when they are facing serious issues. The goal? You don't have any reason to complain about your 'non-serious' problems, while they have every right to keep reminding you of their 'serious' problems. In other words, they want you to shut up and stop complaining about your problems, so they will always be one-up in every situation.

10. They know your emotional buttons and how to press them at will. We all have our emotional weak spots. Emotional manipulators are cleverly aware of your weak spots and do not hesitate to use them for serving their own sinister objectives. They will use knowledge of your weak spots against you.

For example, if you are insecure about your appearance, they will pass snide remarks about everything from your clothes to your weight. Again, if you are worried about an upcoming speech, they will prey on your fears by telling you how tough, picky and judgmental the audience is. They use awareness of your emotions not to make you feel better, but to manipulate you into feeling worse.

11. Emotional manipulators use humor to take a dig at your perceived weaknesses to disempower you or make you feel inadequate. Notice how some people are perpetually making critical or snide remarks about their partner or friend, often in the garb of humor. The idea is to make the other person feel inadequate, inferior or insecure.

Emotional manipulators attempt to disempower the person by playing on his/her perceived weaknesses. The remarks encompass everything from the person's appearance to their old phone to their skills. They make sarcastic and seemingly funny comments about everything, including the fact that you walked in 30 seconds late.

The idea is to make you look bad and feel worse about yourself. This way, the manipulator tries to gain psychological dominance over you, unfortunately, without you even realizing it (now you do, right?). Undermining you makes you perceive yourself as inferior, which automatically gives them the much-needed psychological superiority.

12. Emotional manipulators constantly judge and criticize you to make you feel inferior. In the above example, we saw how manipulators use covert techniques to disempower you by disguising their snide remarks as humor. However, here the emotional manipulator outright dismisses, marginalizes, criticizes and ridicules you in a bid to maintain psychological superiority over you.

Their premise is, if they make you feel inadequate and off-balance, their chances of getting you to do whatever they want increase. You will stop believing in your abilities, sanity and worth, which will help them wield greater control over your thoughts, emotions and actions.

The emotional aggressor will intentionally foster the feeling that something is not right with you, and that, however hard you try, you won't be good enough. Significantly, the emotional manipulator will emphasize on the weaknesses without offering constructive or positive solutions or assisting you in meaningful ways to overcome the negatives.

13. Emotional manipulators will give you the silent treatment. Another art emotional manipulators have mastered is the art of giving people the silent treatment to pressure them into doing what the manipulator wants. They will intentionally make you wait and sow seeds of doubt, insecurity and uncertainty in your mind. Emotional manipulators use silence as leverage to get you to do what they want by keeping you emotionally deprived or insecure.

Being at the receiving end of silent treatment is a warning sign you are dealing with an emotional manipulator. It is a type of emotional abuse through which contempt is demonstrated through nonverbal acts such as remaining silent or withdrawing all communication.

The silent treatment is used as a tool to incite their victims into doing something specific or make them feel inadequate by refusing to acknowledge their presence. If your actions don't match what the manipulator wants you to do, they will utilize the silent treatment for communicating their disappointment and punishing you.

14. Pretend play. Yes, they can play dumb, too, whenever needed. They will pretend that they don't understand what exactly you want or what you desire from them. This is one of the sneaky passive-aggressive tricks where their responsibility becomes yours. So, the bonus of what is essentially their responsibility is

thrown on your shoulders. This is often used by people who are trying to hide something or avoid an obligation.

15. Raising voice and demonstrating negative emotions. Some emotional manipulators know how to use the power of their voice and body language to coerce you into meeting their demands.

They will often raise their voice as a type of aggressive manipulation with the belief that if they sound intimidating enough with their voice, tone and body language, you will invariably submit to their demands. The aggressor-like voice is often combined with intimidating body language such as exaggerated gestures and standing to increase the effect of their aggressive manipulative actions.

16. Negative surprises as a norm. Whoa! Don't these people know how to throw you off balance with their negative surprises in an obvious attempt to gain a psychological advantage over you? They will suddenly come up with some information about not being able to do something or deliver a commitment as promised.

Typically, the negative information is thrown on you without any forewarning to catch you off guard. You are left with no time to come up with a counter move. Emotional manipulators are wolves in sheep's clothing and won't spare a single opportunity to cause discomfort, hurt or harm to you if you get in the way.

CHAPTER TWO

TIPS FOR SPOTTING COVERT MANIPULATION TECHNIQUES

Recognizing covert manipulation tactics is tricky because, unlike overt manipulation, these aren't obvious or in your face. They are often underhanded techniques of trying to gain control of the victim's thoughts, feelings and decisions. It is aimed at bringing down a person's sense of self-worth and destroying their belief in their perceptions. When you learn the manipulator's game, you can play it better than them.

Manipulation undermines the victim's ability to make conscious decisions and act in accordance with their interests. Instead, they become mere puppets in someone else's hands. Manipulators don't value people's personal values, desires and boundaries. In plain words, they'll make you do something you wouldn't normally do.

So, what are the most widely used covert manipulation tactics, and how do you spot them in your everyday life? Read on to de-bluff people's covert manipulation games.

1. They will create a false sense of intimacy. Notice how people are constantly sharing intimate information about themselves in the early stages of a relationship? They will talk about their family, backgrounds and lives (often portraying themselves as victims of circumstances) in a bid to win your sympathy, while also creating an illusion of intimacy.

2. They will introduce other people in the picture in a bid to make you insecure. Again, some people are always trying to create a sense of insecurity or discomfort in their victims by introducing other people into the picture. For example, your partner may talk about meeting an ex-girlfriend/boyfriend or good friend to make you feel insecure.

    Of course, not everyone who meets friends or ex-partners is being manipulative. However, covert manipulators are constantly using this tactic of introducing other people into the picture to unsettle their partner. When a person is trying to pit other people against you to make you feel inadequate, you can be sure it's a covert manipulation tactic.

3. Another covert manipulation technique is 'foot in the door', which is fairly easy to recognize. It involves making a small request that the victim agrees to, which is subsequently followed

by the actual intended request. It is tougher to refuse once the victim agrees to the initial request.

If you refuse the actual request, you'll come across as someone who agrees to something they don't intend to do. When you object to the real request, the manipulator will quickly turn the tables to come across as the aggrieved party. It stops being about their demands since they are now the injured ones. The focus shifts to their complaints, and you are placed on the defensive now. Sometimes, warnings and worry about your well-being are cleverly hidden as concern. Manipulators are forever trying to undermine your choices and decisions in an attempt to shake your self-confidence or sense of self-worth.

4. "Snakes in Suits" – In their publication *Snakes in Suits*, Robert Hare and Paul Babaik advise how people should guard against manipulators who offer out of place and excessive compliments. It is a huge manipulation red flag. Focus keenly on what's next. Keep questioning yourself, *What exactly does this person want from me?*

5. Force Teaming. Have you noticed how some people are always creating a forced sense of team spirit or shared purpose where none exists? Typical phrases used by them include, "We're one team," "How do we handle this as a team?" "We've done it now," etc. They purportedly try to portray that you both are involved in something as a team.

In such a situation, how can you tell if the person is being genuinely helpful or simply trying to manipulate you? Do you feel a strange sense of discomfort while accepting their help? Are their words congruent with their body language? (More on body language later). Is the person giving you an option to refuse help? Are they taking your refusal in the right spirit? If no, you may be dealing with a covert manipulator who is trying to manipulate you under the guise of offering you help.

6. Flattering First Impression. Practiced manipulators often make a stellar first impression. They use a bunch of enticing characteristics such as flawless manners, attractive looks, charismatic smile and courtesy to throw their victims off guard about their real intentions. Yes, they exist beyond the movies, where con men and women are shown to be these stereotypical characters with a dazzling personality and a glib tongue.

    With manipulators, what appears on the surface is not the truth. However, with time and observation, you will notice the cracks in their cleverly worn masks. When it gets really sadistic, the silence is used to torture their victims. For instance, a co-worker talks to everyone at work but ignores you or refuses to have any conversation with you.

7. Covert manipulators will appear to be selfless by keeping their real intentions, ambitions, goals and agendas cleverly cloaked. Their true intentions are hidden under the garb of a selfless cause. This one's tricky to identify. These are the people who

will act like they are working hard on behalf of another person, while hiding their true ambition for power and dominance over others.

For example, a covert manipulator will give his/her manager the impression that they are willing to put in extra hours of work when the manager is away on vacation only to fulfill their ambition of eventually taking over the manager's position.

8. Gas Lighting. The term gas lighting as a covert manipulation technique comes from the play of the same name, which was later adapted into films. It has also been used in literature and psychological research.

    Using the gas lighting technique, a manipulator will twist reality to fulfill their objectives. Irrespective of the truth, they have tricks up their sleeves for making you think that it is indeed your fault for not being able to perceive things correctly. It is so deeply ingrained into your mind that you stop trusting your perceptions and instead accept the manipulator's contrived version of truth. The technique is intended to make you feel so mentally incompetent that you stop trusting your version of reality. It gets to a point where if someone tries to challenge your perceptions, you are mistrustful of them.

9. Rationalization. Rationalization is a technique through which a manipulator offers some form of justification for a hurtful, offensive or inappropriate action. What makes the technique so

tough to spot is that the explanation given often contains enough sense for any reasonable individual to buy it.

Rationalization fulfills three fundamental purposes including, eliminating resistance that manipulators may have about their inappropriate action, keeping others from pointing fingers at them and helping the manipulator justify his/her actions in the victim's eyes.

Manipulators who use rationalization will typically behave very affectionately at times and then suddenly act distant or cold. When the victim gets tired of their behavior and confronts them or avoids them, they will most likely scream or cry. They will mention how they have been depressed or upset of late and how you are such a bad person for confronting them about their seemingly inappropriate behavior when you are one who is behaving insensitively.

They will move you to tears with how stressful their life is, even apologize for it at times. However, within the next few days, they'll repeat the pattern. Manipulators are remarkable performers. They can play the victim's role with ease. They can fake emotions, cry at will, laugh when they want to and pretend to be sad or happy on demand. Carefully examine the acts of people who 'love you' or forever try to gain sympathy.

10. Nitpicking and goal post moving. The difference between positive criticism and negative/destructive criticism is a manipulator will come up with near impractical standards and

personal attacks. These self-proclaimed critics pretend to help your development, when in fact, they don't want to see you improve. They are simply operating with the intention of nitpicking at you, pulling you down and making you a scapegoat in every possible manner.

Covert manipulators are masters in the art of 'moving goalposts' to ensure they are never short of reasons to be disappointed with you. Even when you present evidence to validate your stand or act to fulfill their request, they will come up with another lofty expectation for you to meet or ask for more proof to validate your argument. Yes, who said dealing with manipulators was easy?

For example, they may start by picking on you for not having a successful career. When you have a successful career, they'll question you for not being a multi-millionaire yet. When that expectation is met, they'll demand to know why your personal/work life is never balanced. The goal posts will keep changing, and the expectations will rise higher in a bid to make you feel incompetent in some way or the other.

One of the easiest ways to spot a manipulator is to observe if they are constantly instilling a sense of unworthiness in you or forever making you feel whatever you do is never good enough. A genuine or constructive person will never induce a sense of unworthiness in you. They will gently point out your limitations and often suggest ways to overcome them. Manipulators, on the other hand, will never offer suggestions to help you overcome your limitations.

If a person is constantly criticizing you without helping you overcome the issue or limitations in a meaningful way, you may likely be a victim of covert manipulation. They will cleverly present it as constructive criticism even if it's just nitpicking without offering solutions.

If a person keeps demanding more proof for validating your argument or keeps raising their expectations, their aim is obviously not to understand you better. They are attempting to provoke you into experiencing a sense of inadequacy or that you have to keep proving yourself all the time.

11. Withholding apology. Covert manipulators will seldom apologize for their actions. Instead they will deny, lie or shift the blame to avoid accepting responsibility for their act. Be mindful of this covert manipulation technique by examining if the person apologizes and accepts responsibility for their mistakes.

If a person constantly makes you feel like you are blowing things out of proportion or overreacting rather than apologizing, you are probably dealing with a covert manipulator. Manipulators have a strong urge to be right, even at the cost of mending a relationship. Withholding apology is just another controlling mechanism for them.

12. Undermining your success. I once had a friend who was constantly made to feel guilty by his partner about being successful. He was creating a promising future for them and their future kids, but she constantly made him feel terrible about the fact that he worked so hard and barely had time for her. She accused him of being selfish and thinking only about his goals, when in fact, he was building a future for their family.

When you tell your partner or a close friend about a promotion or a new job offer, how should they usually react? They should be delighted you are progressing in life. Those who truly care about you will want to see you succeed. Manipulators will constantly try to underplay and undermine your success. They will always find some way to instill negativity in any form related to your success story. This arises from a clear sense of insecurity that you are now becoming more self-sufficient and will no longer need them.

The feeling that the more successful you become, the less they'll be able to control you leads them to behave in an irrational manner. Thus, they'll make you feel miserable about your success. Sometimes, they'll even get angry for no apparent reason. One of their biggest concerns is that financial independence will give you the ability to survive without their help. This prospect can be threatening for a person who is accustomed to having his/her friend or partner depend on him/her excessively.

CHAPTER THREE

WHY MANIPULATORS MANIPULATE

Now that you are fairly competent in identifying emotional and covert manipulation tactics, let's understand what leads people to manipulate others. This may help you deal with them more efficiently.

We've all been victims of everything from pathological lying to being made to feel inadequate to suffering awful smear campaigns. They are beyond reasonable standards of human behavior. What makes people turn into sinister manipulators? What leads manipulators to use the tactics they do? What makes them defy norms of human behavior and turn to underhanded techniques to have their way with people?

Read on to get deeper insights about what makes people manipulate others in ways you'd never imagine.

Fear

Why does a person use manipulation to fulfill his/her own agenda? Simple - fear!

It is obvious that manipulators fear that they will never be able to gain the desired outcome on their own abilities. That if they act ethically, people and life will not reward them positively. They operate from the view that people are life, and people are positioned against them. Manipulators fear everyone as their enemy and believe life will not necessarily be favorable to them if they act favorably.

There is a fear that resources are limited, and if they don't gain something, others will. They think it's a dog-eat-dog universe where people must be controlled to help them accomplish the desired result. This control can be in any form – emotional, psychological, financial or practical. They want to control people, so they can achieve their desired agenda and put their fear to rest.

Manipulators are constantly living under fear and insecurity. 'What if this doesn't happen?' 'What if my partner leaves me for someone else?' 'What if someone gains an upper hand over me?' They want to win and control all the time to combat an inherent sense of fear.

Where does this fear stem from? It originates from a deep sense of unworthiness. This simply translates as 'I am certainly not worthy of the good things and people in life, hence, these things and people will leave me. To prevent them from leaving me, I must resort to some underhanded techniques that will give me absolute control over the people and things I believe I don't deserve.' In short, the underlying message is – 'I am undeserving or unworthy of people and things!'

Low or No Conscience

Lack of conscience is another fundamental reason for manipulation. When a person fails to realize that he/she is responsible for their own reality, there is a greater tendency to operate without a conscience. Manipulators don't believe a fair system exists. Also, they've stopped evolving. They don't learn from earlier experiences or try to accomplish a state of congruence between inner emotions and external life.

They view manipulation as a safe or secure world for getting the desired result, despite the fact that these results have not brought them satisfaction in the past. Emotionally and psychologically, they keep coming back to square one from time to time, never learning their lesson. To avoid this lesson, they will create another reason to manipulate. Thus, they are caught in vicious circle of unworthiness or dissatisfaction, thus, creating another manipulation need.

Manipulation doesn't pay beyond the initial brief fix since the manipulative action is not authentic, balanced or effective. It is a defense reaction to perceived hurt, unworthiness, fear or insecurity. By being manipulative, the person is attempting to offset these emotions.

Manipulation is a deliberate act that is not aligned with a person's conscience or greater good. The person doesn't operate with a "we are one" understanding, which means he/she seeks to gain through manipulation by authenticity rather than non-authenticity. Anything gained through non-authenticity only leads to narrow victories, ongoing trouble, emptiness or fear and unworthiness. This creates an even bigger sense of unworthiness. Again, unworthiness is a fear of not being worthy of others' love and acceptance.

Manipulative folks do not learn, evolve or realize the power of authenticity. Lack of realization of the real power of authenticity and worthiness comes from knowing that one is cherished and accepted for what they really are. In essence, a feeling of unworthiness is often at the core of manipulation.

They Don't Want to Pay the Price Attached to Reach Their Goals

People often manipulate to serve their needs because they do not want to pay the price attached to their goal. They often strive to accomplish the objective or serve their purpose without wanting to give back or pay the price in return.

For instance, if you don't want your partner to leave you, the relationship will take work. You'll have to give your partner love, compassion, understanding, time, loyalty, encouragement, inspiration, a secure future and much more.

A manipulator may not want his/her partner to leave them, but they don't want to pay the price of maintaining a happy, secure and healthy relationship, whereby the partner will never leave them. They may not want to be loyal or spend much time with their partner, and yet they expect them to stay. When people are not ready to pay the price of accomplishing what they want, they may resort to manipulation or underhanded techniques to achieve these goals without paying the price attached to them.

Similarly, if a manipulative person wants to be promoted in his/her workplace, rather than working hard, staying past work hours, upgrading their skills or getting a degree, they will simply manipulate their way into the position. The person is not prepared to pay the price or do what it takes to be promoted.

At times, it's deeply ingrained in a person's psyche that wants are bad or that he/she shouldn't have any desires since it makes them come across as selfish. Manipulation then becomes a way to get what they desire or need without even asking for it.

Manipulators realize there is a price attached to everything. A person won't do them a favor without expecting a favor in return. They won't keep getting things if they don't demonstrate kindness and gratitude. A person won't love them or have sex with them without getting commitment, loyalty and love in return. Manipulators try to push their luck by trying to get something without paying the price attached to it. It is often the easy way out.

They Think They Won't Get Caught

Another reason people manipulate is because they think they can get away with their sneaky acts and that the victims won't realize they are being manipulated. They are also confident that the victim can't do anything even if their manipulation cover is blown.

What gives manipulators the feeling that they won't be caught? Some people come across as inherently clueless, vulnerable, insecure and naïve. These are the type of people manipulators prey on. They believe a person who has low confidence, a low sense of self-worth or is clueless about the ways of the world is less likely to figure out that he/she is being manipulated.

Also, manipulators know that in the event that their manipulation cover is blown, the victim will not be able to do much. They cleverly pick targets who are low in confidence, self-acceptance, body image or sense of self-worth. It is easier to play on the vulnerabilities of these people than on assertive and self-assured people who won't allow people to take advantage of them.

For example, say a person has low awareness of social dynamics, doesn't understand jokes easily, doesn't identify a prank early, is unable to differentiate between genuine courtesy and sexual advances, can't tell when someone is genuinely attracted to them or simply wants to go to bed with them and other similar social and interpersonal dynamics. That person is more likely to be manipulated.

Manipulators are well aware that their victims can't do anything if they don't even realize that their weaknesses are being misused. They often cash in on the cluelessness of their victims by saying they are imagining things or making something up. An already clueless and unsure person is less likely to question this idea. When you are already reeling under feelings of insecurity, cluelessness and vulnerability, how difficult is it for a manipulator to take advantage of these feelings by reinforcing them further?

Manipulators

Manipulators manipulate because they think they can hurt or upset their victims more than the victims can hurt or upset them. They will almost always target people who come across as nice and vulnerable. When people are oblivious to the dishonesty existing within social relationships, they aren't really accustomed to dishonest allegiances. This doesn't equip them with the means to confront or counter dishonesty, which makes them less aware of being manipulated.

They Aren't Able to Accept Their Shortcomings

When people are unable to come to terms with their shortcomings or do not accept the responsibility or accountability for their faults, there is an inherent need to make others feel lesser than them.

If manipulators aren't good enough or feel miserable about themselves, there is a desire to make others feel equally worthless or miserable about themselves. When a person believes he/she is unworthy of someone, they will manipulate the person to feel unworthy, too. They can then gain control over his/her perception that they need the manipulator in their life to feel worthy. By putting others down or gaining control over others, they experience a form of pseudo superiority. If they can't be good enough for others, they make others feel like they aren't good enough to retain control over them.

In effect, manipulators don't want their victims to realize that they (the manipulators) aren't good enough or unworthy of them (the victims). The manipulator will therefore carefully cultivate a feeling of helplessness and unworthiness within the victim to keep them hooked to him/her. If a person realizes that he/she is more attractive, intelligent, richer, capable, efficient, self-sufficient etc., the higher their chances will be of leaving the manipulator. On the other hand, if the manipulator injects a feeling of the person not being 'complete,' they'll need someone to 'complete' them.

Manipulators are not able to accept their shortcomings or deal with criticism. They are often grappling with deep psychological issues or insecurities. By manipulating others, they do not have to confront their own insecurities to feel higher than others. For someone operating with such a narrow perspective, even a little correction, feedback or criticism can seem like a huge defeat.

People who manipulate don't know how to deal with defeat. When you hesitate to give feedback because the person will get defensive or blow things out of proportion or won't take things in the right spirit, it may be a sign you are dealing with someone who can't come to terms with criticism.

Notice how manipulators will seldom express feelings of gratitude or thankfulness. They find it challenging to be grateful to others because, in their view, by doing so they are increasing their sense of being obligated to another person, which doesn't give them an upper hand in any relationship.

For example, if you do someone a huge favor, they feel obliged to return that favor, which puts you above them in the relationship dynamics until they return the favor. Manipulators don't want to give you the upper hand by feeling obliged to you. Therefore, they will demonstrate minimal gratefulness, so you don't believe you've done something huge for them or that they are obliged to you. The idea is to always be one-up on you, and this feeling of being indebted to you doesn't make them feel one-up.

CHAPTER FOUR

MANIPULATION AND NEURO LINGUISTIC PROGRAMMING

What is Neuro Linguistic Programming?

Neuro Linguistic Programming, or NLP, in simplest terms is the programming language of your mind. We've all had instances where we attempted to communicate with someone who doesn't speak our language. The outcome? They didn't understand us!

You go to a restaurant abroad and ask for a fancy steak but end up receiving insipid stew owing to the misinterpretation of language and codes.

This is precisely what happens when we try to communicate with our subconscious mind. We think we are commanding it to give us happier relationships, more money, a better job and other, similar things. However, if that's not what is actually showing up, something is being lost in translation. The subconscious/unconscious mind has the power to help us accomplish our goals only if we program it using codes it recognizes and understands.

If you are asking your unconscious mind for steak and receiving stew, it is time to speak its language. Think of NLP as a user manual for the brain. When people master NLP, they become fluent in the language of the subconscious mind, which is excellent when it comes to re-programming their own and other people's thoughts, ideas and beliefs. This gives them the power to influence and persuade people, and on the downside, even manipulate them.

Neuro Linguistic Programming is a set of techniques, methods and tools for enhancing communication with deeper layers of our brain. It is an approach that combines personal development, psychotherapy and communication. Its creators (John Grinder and Richard Bandler) claim that there is a strong link between language, behavior patterns and neurological processes, which can be used for enhancing learning and personal development.

Influence versus Manipulation

So, do you believe a hammer is a tool of utility or destruction? Well, it depends on how you use it, right? Or what purpose you use it for.

NLP is potent when it comes to getting people to do what you want them to. It is the hammer that can be used to fix a nail in the wall or destroy a piece of wood. Similarly, NLP can be used to build something positive, or it can be used for a destructive purpose (manipulation).

NLP and manipulation have nearly the same meaning. Both are about generating the desired effect on other people without obvious exertion. However, one key difference between influence and manipulation is that the latter is meant to influence others to meet the manipulator's selfish goals through means that can be unfair, unlawful, sneaky, or insidious. Things are contrived through underhanded methods to turn out in favor of the manipulator. A manipulator often preys on the insecurities, fears and guilt of other people. In turn, victims of manipulation feed dissatisfied, frustrated, trapped and unhappy.

Conversely, influence is the ability to inspire people in an admirable, charismatic and honorable way. We are often inspired by influential people and aspire to model our life on theirs. There is a general feeling of positivity related to them, and we feel positively impacted in their company. Not every influence is positive, which is why we use terms such as "bad influence" to signify a person's negative effect on us. However, manipulation is never categorized as good or bad. It always operates with sinister motives. That is the primary difference between influence and manipulation.

Influence is a double-edged sword that can be used positively and negatively, while manipulation only operates with a negative, narrow and selfish perspective to meet the objectives of the manipulator.

While manipulation has self-centered and questionable motives, influence can also be positive. In contrast to manipulation, influence has positive connotations, which considers other people's needs, goals and desires. Don't we, as parents, want to influence our children to lead happier and healthier lives? Similarly, as a manager, we want to influence our team to put in their best efforts.

Just like the hammer discussed above, people can use NLP for positively or negatively influencing people to meet their own selfish objectives (manipulation). NLP is a mind control tool that can do both – build and damage.

How is NLP Used for Manipulating People?

NLP training is conducted in a pyramid-like structure, with sophisticated techniques reserved for high-end seminars. It is a complex subject (whoever said anything related to the human mind would be easy?). However, to simplify a complicated concept, NLPers, or people who practice NLP, pay keen attention to people they work with. They watch everything from eye movements to skin flushes to pupil dilation in order to determine what type of information people are processing.

Through observation, NLPers can tell which side of the brain is dominant in a person. Similarly, they can tell what sense is the most active within the person's brain. The eye movements can determine how their brain stores and uses information. It is also easy to decipher whether the person is stating facts (telling the truth) or making up facts (lying) by looking at his/her eye movements.

After gathering this invaluable information, NLP manipulators will subtly mirror and mimic their victims (including speech, body language, mannerisms, verbal linguistic patterns and more) to give a feeling of being 'one among them.'

NLPers will fake social clues to lead their victims into dropping their guard and entering a more open, receptive and suggestible state of mind, where they become ready to absorb whatever information their mind is fed. Manipulators will cleverly use language that focuses on a person's predominant senses.

For example, if a person is focused on his/her visual sense, the NLP manipulator will most likely use it to his/her advantage optimally by saying something like, "Do you see where I am coming from?" "Can you see what I am trying to tell you?" or "See it this way?" Similarly, if a person is a predominantly auditory person, the manipulator will speak to them using auditory metaphors like, "Just hear me out once, Tim" or "I hear you."

By mirroring their victim's body language and verbal linguistic patterns, NLP experts, or NLPer manipulators, attempt to accomplish a clear objective – building rapport. As discussed earlier, manipulators also try to accomplish this by sharing too much too soon or building early intimacy. The objective is the same

– to strike a rapport with their victims, which then makes it easy for the victims to let down their guard.

Once the manipulator uses NLP to build rapport and get the victim to let down his guard through clever use of body language and verbal patterns, the victim becomes more open and suggestible. Fake social cues are fed to the victim to make their minds more malleable.

Once they build a rapport, NLPers will begin to lead the victim into increased interaction in a sublime manner. After having mirrored the victim and establishing in the victim's subconscious mind that he/she (the manipulator) is one among them (the victim), the manipulator increases his/her chances of getting the victim to do whatever the manipulator wants. They will subtly change their behavior and language to influence their victim's actions.

The techniques can include leading questions, sublime language patterns and a host of other NLP techniques to maneuver the person's mind wherever they want. The victim, on the other hand, often doesn't realize what is happening. In their view, everything is occurring naturally/organically or according to their consent.

Of course, manipulators (however skilled) may not be able to use NLP to get people to behave in a manner that is completely out of character. However, it can be used to steer people's responses in the desired direction. For instance, you can't convince a fundamentally ethical and truthful person to act in a dishonest manner. However, you can use it to get a person to think in a specific direction or line of thought. Manipulators use NLP to engineer specific responses from a person.

NLP attempts accomplish two ends, eliciting and anchoring. Eliciting occurs when NLPers use language and leading to draw their victims into an emotional state. Once the desired state is accomplished, the NLPer will then anchor the emotion with a specific physical clue - for example, tapping on their shoulder. This simply means that an NLPer can invoke the same emotion in you by tapping your shoulder.

For example, let us say the NLP manipulator makes you feel depressed or unworthy using language, leading and other NLP techniques. This is followed by tapping the back of your hands in a specific manner to create anchoring. Thus, each time they want to create an emotion of being disillusioned, depressed and unworthy in you, they will tap the back of your palm. It is nothing but conditioning you to feel in a certain way with linked physical clues.

Now that you have a fair idea of what NLP is or how manipulators can use it for submission, what can you do to guard yourself against NLP manipulators?

Here are some tips to prevent NLPers from pulling their remarkably smart yet sneaky tricks on you:

1. Be wary of people mirroring your body language. Agreed, you didn't know this until now, but people imitating or copying your body language is one of the biggest red flags of them trying to

manipulate, influence or persuade you to act in a desired manner. I really enjoy testing these NLP experts using subtle hand gestures and leg movements to gauge if they are indeed mirroring my body language to establish a rapport.

If they follow suit, that's my clue to flee! Experienced NLPers have mastered the art of subtle mirroring, which means you may not even realize they are imitating your actions. NLP beginners will instantly imitate the exact same movement in their eagerness to establish a feeling of oneness. Good way for you to call their bluff!

2. Confuse with eye movements. Another fantastic way to call an NLP manipulator's bluff is to notice if they are paying very close attention to your eyes or eye movements. NLP users often examine their target or victim's very carefully. The eye movements are scrutinized to gauge how you access and store information.

In effect, they want to determine what parts of the brain you are utilizing to gather clues about your thoughts and feelings. I say beat this by darting your eyes all around the place randomly. Move them upwards and downwards or from side to side in no clear pattern. You are throwing your NLP manipulator off course. Make it appear natural. Their calibration will go down the wayside.

3. Beware of people's touch. As we discussed earlier, one of the techniques NLPers use is anchoring. If you know a person

practices NLP, and you are in an especially heightened or intense emotional condition, do not allow them to touch you in any manner. Just throw them off course by suddenly laughing hard or flying into a fit of rage. Basically, you are confusing them about the emotion they need to anchor. Even if they attempt to establish a physical clue to invoke certain emotions, they'll be left with a mixed bag of crazy laughter, rage and whatever else you did.

4. Watch out for permissive language. Typical language used by NLPers includes "be relaxed," "relax and enjoy this," and other similar statements. Beware of this NLP, hypnotist style language that induces you into a state of deep relaxation or trance to get you to think or act in a specific manner. Skilled or covert manipulators rarely command in a straightforward manner.

    They will cleverly seek your permission to give you the impression that you are doing what they want you to do out of your own free will (one of their many sinister tricks). If you observe experienced hypnotists, they will never outright command you to do anything but seek your permission to make it appear as if it is being done organically, with your consent.

5. Guard Against Gibberish. Watch out for mumbo jumbo that just doesn't make any logical sense or twisted/complicated statements that mean little. For example, "As you free the feeling of being held by your thoughts, you will find yourself in alignment with the voice of your success." Does this make any

sense? NLP manipulators won't say anything purposeful, but rather, they will program your emotional state to lead it where they want to.

One of the best ways to guard against this sort of hypnotism-NLP induced manipulation is to urge the manipulator to be more specific. "Can you be clearer about this?" "Can you specify exactly what you mean by that?" It won't just interrupt their cleverly set technique but will also force the interaction into precise language, thus breaking the trance brought about through ambiguous words and phrases.

6. Don't quickly agree to anything. If you find yourself being compelled to make an instant decision about something important, and it feels like you are steered in a specific direction, escape the situation. Wait a day to make a decision. Do not be swept or led into making a decision that you do not want to make on an impulse. Sales professionals are adept at manipulating buyers into purchasing something they don't need using sneaky manipulation and NLP tactics. When someone rushes you into a decision, it should be a warning signal to back off and hold on until you've thought more about the situation.

CHAPTER FIVE

TECHNIQUES FOR OUTSMARTING MANIPULATORS

Like it or wince, the world is full of wolves in sheep's clothing. You can't do much about pathological and emotional manipulators who are out to leverage your feelings and emotions to satisfy their wants. However, you can beat them in their own game by using a bunch of outsmarting techniques. Manipulation, if not recognized and handled efficiently, can tear down your sense of self-worth and sanity. By recognizing and coping with manipulation, you are standing up for yourself and not allowing sinister manipulators to fulfill their agenda by tramping on your feelings.

Here are some smart and effective hacks for outsmarting manipulators in their own game:

1. Put the spotlight on them by posing probing queries. Manipulators are constantly demanding things or making offers to their victims. As a victim, you will be made to feel that you

need to prove yourself all the time. You'll often go out of the way to fulfill these demands. Stop. Each time you find them coming up with an unreasonable request, shoot back a few probing questions and shift the focus on them.

For example, Does this seem like a legitimate and reasonable request to you?

Do you think what you've asked from me is fair or ethical?

Do I have the right to refuse?

Are you requesting or demanding that I do this?

What do I gain from doing this?

Are you really expecting that I will do this?

Are you reasonably justified in expecting me to do this?

Who stands to gain the most from this?

Basically, you ask questions that show them the mirror, where they can witness their real, sinister ploy. If the manipulator is self-aware or realizes that you've seen through their motives, they will most likely withdraw the request.

Manipulators try to put the focus on you as if you are unworthy or 'bad' if you don't do something for them. You've got to put the focus back on them by making them think whether their request is indeed justified or reasonable, thus, making them come across as people with evil motives.

Questions will eventually force the manipulator to realize that you are seeing through their game. The focus of the action will now shift from you to them.

For example, if you refuse the manipulator's request, the onus of justifying your action isn't on you. By asking probing questions, you are asking the manipulator to justify the reasonability of their request. So, instead of feeling guilty about refusing something, you are making the manipulator realize that he/she is at fault for having unreasonable expectations.

Also, let your manipulator know that you don't accept being treated the way they treat you. Make it sufficiently clear that you don't appreciate their ways.

For instance, if you are already preoccupied with something, and the manipulator makes a request to do something for them, say something to the effect that, "I do not appreciate it when I am already working on something and you make another request of me before I finish the current task."

Similarly, when a person is trying to force you into making a decision that benefits them, say something like, "I am able to make my own decisions and would really appreciate if you don't coerce me into making a decision in a hurry." You are being assertive and telling off your manipulator without being rude.

You are simply standing up for your right and informing them that you have the right to take your time to decide, and it could backfire if they pressure you into making a decision.

2. Take your time in fulfilling a request. Not only will manipulators make unreasonable requests, they will also pressure you into making a quick decision. They want to wield optimal control, influence and pressure over you to get you to act in a specific way immediately. Manipulators realize that if you take more time, things may not go in their favor.

   Do the exact opposite of what they want by taking more time. Sales people are always focused on closing the deal soon. Distance yourself from the manipulator's persuasion and take time to arrive at a decision. You don't have to act right away, however much the person tries to pressure you.

   Take control over the person and situation by saying something like, "I'd like more time to think about it" or "It is my right to take more time to think about a decision as important as this" or "I need to evaluate the pros and cons before I arrive at a decision."

   You can use this time to negotiate in your favor.

3. Say no assertively yet diplomatically. This is an art which will only come with practice. You don't want to offend the manipulator by saying a straight no. Yet, you want to be firm and let them know you won't allow them to walk all over you.

Stand your ground, while still being polite and courteous. You don't have to feel guilty about your right to refuse an unreasonable request.

If you aren't up for something, say, "I understand you want me to do this, but I also feel I am not up for it right now." Another way to articulate your needs is, "The best thing for me to do right now is..." One of the best comebacks is to focus on your needs over those of the manipulator without guilt.

One of the sneakiest tricks used by manipulators is to make you feel guilty every time you don't comply with their request. When you stop feeling guilty about standing up for yourself or exercising your right to be treated with respect, manipulators become powerless.

4. Know your fundamental rights and worth. The most important weapon when you are dealing with manipulators is to know when your rights are being violated. You have the absolute right to stand up for those rights and defend yourself. You have the fundamental right to be treated with respect and honor.

Again, you have the right to express your emotions, needs and feelings. You have the right to establish your priorities, refuse something without feeling guilty, the right to protect yourself/love ones from harm, the right to acquire what you pay for, and the right to live a happy, healthy and fulfilling life.

These are your boundaries, and you can remind people to respect these rights. Psychological manipulators often want to take away your fundamental rights in a bid to exercise greater control over you. However, the power and authority to take charge of your life lies with you, and you shouldn't miss an opportunity to remind your manipulator that you alone are in control of your life. Distance yourself from people who do not respect these basic boundaries.

5. Maintain your distance. One of the most effective ways to spot a manipulator is by observing how they act differently with different folks or in diverse situations. Of course, we all come with some amount of social differential, but if the person is habitually behaving out of character in extremes, he/she may be a master manipulator.

Think, being unnaturally polite to one person and the next minute downright rude to another or acting vulnerable one moment and then becoming aggressive within the next. When you witness this type of behavior, maintain your distance from the person. Avoid interacting with these people until absolutely necessary. Otherwise, you may end up inviting trouble. There are plenty of reasons people manipulate, and it is very psychologically complex. Don't attempt to fix manipulators all the time. It isn't your duty to change them. Just save yourself by moving on.

6. Avoid blaming yourself, or personalization. One of the smoothest tricks used by manipulators is to make their victims feel like it is always their (the victim's) fault. Irrespective of what the manipulator does or knows, they will never take accountability for their faults. They will always blame the victim for all their wrongs.

As a victim of manipulation, you need to stop personalizing. The problem is not with you since you are simply being made to feel that it's your fault, so you give away your rights to the manipulator and become powerless.

Do not be led into thinking that you are the problem, or the problem lies with you. I knew a friend who was constantly chided by her husband for working hard to support the family. He never missed an opportunity to remind her that she wasn't a good wife or mother because she was always working. In her mind, she was working hard to give her children a great future (which really didn't make her a bad mother).

However, in his attempt to gain absolute control over her, he constantly blamed her and made her feel incompetent as a wife and mother. Initially, my friend believed everything that was told to her about being a bad mother and wife. However, over a period of time, she realized she was simply being blamed because her husband couldn't come to terms with his own shortcomings.

Ask yourself these questions before blaming yourself:

Are you being treated with respect?

Are the person's demands reasonable?

Do I feel good about myself while interacting with this person?

These are important clues about the real problem.

7. Set consequences for manipulative behavior. Psychological and pathological manipulators will always insist on disregarding your rights. They rarely take no for an answer, often flying into a rage or becoming aggressive. Recognize and state consequences clearly if they resort to aggression as a response to your refusal to comply with their unreasonable request.

An effectively communicated and asserted consequence can be used to pin down a manipulative person and compel him/her to change their stand from violating your rights to respecting them. By reinforcing consequences, you are uncovering their hidden agendas and making them bring about a shift in their attitude towards you. Basically, you are cutting off their power.

It is important to stand up against the manipulator's bullying tactics. They will often try to scare you into giving in to their demands. Manipulators claim to hold on to your weaknesses to feel superior and powerful. If you stay passive and play along, they'll take greater advantage of you. Confront them and exercise your rights. Since manipulators are inherently cowardly, they'll retreat.

Research has proven that being manipulative is closely linked to an abusive childhood or being victims of bullying. This in no way justifies the act of a bully. However, when you keep this in mind, you'll find healthier and more effective ways to respond to the manipulator.

8. Value yourself for who you are. Manipulators feed on the low self-esteem of their victims. They'll always catch people who are vulnerable, unsure, low on confidence and don't know their real worth.

   Rarely will the manipulator go after people with a high self-esteem or sense of self-worth. If you can stay strong and take the manipulator head on by establishing your self-worth, it is evident you won't allow anyone to control you.

9. Silence is golden. Manipulators love drama. They will often provoke feelings of anger, fear, sadness and more in you to think they've scored points over you. The best way to deal with this is to stay calm and practice deep breathing. Concentrate on your breath and how the body feels. Try to relax your muscles and look the manipulator in the eye.

   This simple body language of confidence and assertion can throw them off the tangent. A manipulator doesn't know how to deal with your calmness in such a situation. They are fully equipped to deal with your anger and fear. However, they don't expect you to react with calmness. It infuriates them and tells them the ploy doesn't seem to be effective on you. They will learn that your emotions remain unchanged and shift to another target.

Don't get me wrong here. I am certainly not advocating giving up on a relationship at the first sign of manipulation. Manipulation can slowly pop up even in otherwise happy and fulfilling relationships, and it doesn't necessarily signify the end of a relationship. Before taking any drastic step, have a frank and open conversation with your partner or the person who is manipulating you. Gather the courage to ask them why they are doing this to you. These answers may give you vital clues into their state of mind and your next move.

If you've already attempted to have an open communication with your partner and they wouldn't have any of it, it may be time to explore other options such as therapy or counseling. However, you both have to be committed to the pursuit of overcoming manipulation within the relationship.

10. Practice self-care. Coping with a manipulative relationship can be intensely exhausting and stressful. Ensure you practice self-care to nurture your mind, body and spirit, and don't let the manipulation take its toll on you. It is common to feel stressed at the end of each interaction with a manipulator (been there, done that).

When you feel your mental energy drained after communication with a manipulator, do meditation, yoga or deep breathing. It infuses a sense of calm into your being. Do something enjoyable and exciting to prevent the negative feelings from spoiling your day. Go for a long walk in the midst of nature or talk to someone you trust.

57

CHAPTER SIX

DEALING WITH MANIPULATION IN RELATIONSHIPS

Emotional manipulation or being in a manipulative relationship is one of the most unfortunate things a person can experience. Not only does it destroy your sense of self-worth, but it also prevents you from enjoying fulfilling and rewarding relationships in the future. Manipulation goes against the ethos of a healthy, happy, positive and inspiring relationship.

While we are all in some way or another manipulating our loved ones, it becomes sinister when it hits at a person's emotions or sense of self-worth for fulfilling a selfish agenda. Here are some effective deals for dealing with manipulation in relationships:

1. Closely observe your feelings after every interaction. Do a majority of your conversations or interactions with your partner make you feel confused, unworthy or overcome by self-

doubt? By doing a routine check of your feelings, you will be able to identify a clear cause.

For example, if you realize that you always feel guilty after a conversation with your partner, rewind to the conversation and go over what your partner said after each interaction. How did it start? What are the typical words and phrases they use while talking to you? Is there a pattern to what they say and how they make you feel?

It would be even better if you can make a note of your feelings to easily identify the emerging pattern.

Tell yourself that the problem is them and not you. Remember that you are only being hoodwinked into thinking it is your fault or you aren't good enough. The manipulator is most likely dealing with grave issues of their own, which they are incapable of handling effectively. This is only to help you establish a context for their acts, not to make you feel sympathetic towards them. Keep in mind, manipulators seldom deserve sympathy!

2. Assess your relationship objectively. If you can't determine if you are truly in a manipulative relationship, get a reality check by talking to friends or people you trust.

Ask them for an objective assessment of your relationship frankly. Do they think your partner has unreasonable expectations of you? Do they think your partner is taking advantage of you? Do they think you are being emotionally vulnerable?

Sometimes, by talking to a third person, we gain a perspective we hadn't considered before. It'll probably give you a new way of looking at things, which will allow you to act immediately if you are being manipulated.

3. Confront the manipulator. Consider various angles before approaching and confronting your manipulator. They most likely won't admit to their manipulative acts, especially if you sound unsure and nervous.

    Rather than making statements about how they have been "using you" or "taking advantage of you," get down to specifics. How does a specific action or certain words make you feel? List specific instances where you felt you were taken advantage of. Follow this up with a positive and gentle, yet assertive, request to mend their behavior.

    You are communicating to the manipulator that you are aware of their tricks, which makes them more cautious while manipulating you. In the same vein, you are also giving them an opportunity to get their act together. It will take real effort and commitment on your part to move out of an emotionally manipulative relationship. You will have to stay vigilant and develop limitless reserves of self-esteem and positivity.

4. Hit hard at the center of their gravity. If nothing else seems to work, hit the manipulator hard at his/her center of gravity. They'll often resort to evil strategies such as befriending your friends and then speaking evil about you or tempting you with a reward and then backing off or not honoring their commitment.

    Since you know the person inside out, hit them where it hurts the most. Their center may be their friends, followers or anything they think is integral to their existence. Use this knowledge to beat them at their own game.

5. Don't fit in with their ideas. The key to avoid being manipulated is to reinvent yourself and have your own ideas about things rather than subscribing to theirs. Manipulators will shove their ideas down your throat since they need to control you to further their agenda. Have your own clear views, ideas and opinions about various aspects of your life. Consistently drilling a particular idea into your mind is how they are able to successfully confine you in a box.

    Don't try to fit in, focus on reinvention. Work hard towards standing out from the rest. Be different, unique and remarkable in your own way. Personal growth and building your self-esteem is the key for fighting manipulation.

6. Don't compromise. Guilt is a powerful emotion leveraged by manipulators. They will use your self-doubt and guilt to their advantage. The agenda is to tip your sense of balance and instill

a sense of uncertainty within you. This uncertainty eventually drives you to compromise on your values, ideals and goals.

Avoid feeling guilty or compromising. Don't doubt yourself or your abilities. Even though you are in a relationship with a person, you don't owe them anything if you are not treated with respect. Every person deserves to feel wonderful and positive about themselves. If a person doesn't make you feel good about yourself or your accomplishments, there may be a problem. Have a firm belief in your values and ideals. Don't compromise on your values, beliefs, goals and ideals. Remember, you deserve to feel great about yourself and your achievements. There should be a strong sense of self-belief, self-assuredness and confidence in what you are doing.

A manipulator becomes powerless in the face of high self-confidence. They start losing their influence once you learn to operate with confidence and refuse to compromise on anything that undermines your self-respect or core values.

7. Don't seek permission. This is like handing the manipulator the pass to manipulate you as they wish. The trouble is, since childhood, we've been conditioned to seek permission. As an infant, we seek permission to eat and sleep. All through school we are seeking permission to visit the bathroom, eat our lunch or drink water.

A direct consequence of this is, even as grown-ups, we don't stop seeking permission from people close to us. Instead of informing your partner you are planning to meet a friend over lunch, you'll subconsciously ask them if it is alright if you plan something with your friend. By constantly and habitually seeking permission, you are only giving the control of your life to someone else, especially if he/she is a more manipulative type.

Don't be overly concerned about being polite or making others feel good at the cost of your own comfort and happiness. Remember, you have the right to live your life exactly the way you want to. Emotional manipulation is about making you feel beholden or enslaved by some imaginary rule that exists only in the mind of the manipulator. They'll never want you to feel self-sufficient and make your own decisions because that diminishes their hold over you.

There's no need to bow to their authoritative dictates or consult them before everything you do, unless it does impact them in an important manner. I happened to have a co-worker who would seek his girlfriend's permission even before going for a coffee break or out for lunch. It was ridiculous the way she treated him and tried to control every move of his. Predictably, the relationship ended on a sour note.

However, no one can make you feel miserable without your permission. And by constantly seeking permission, you are giving your partner the permission to make you feel miserable – if that makes sense. You can disregard the manipulator's obsession with confining you anytime by living your life the way you want to, without their interference or permission.

8. Be open to new opportunities. The manipulator wants you to put all your eggs in their basket, so they can throw away the basket whenever they fancy. Don't lock yourself into them or be tied down by a commitment you aren't comfortable making. Don't be content or accept your current life. If you are in a highly manipulative or emotionally/physically abusive relationship, attempt to break free and explore other relationships or opportunities.

Manipulators in relationships often take advantage of the fact that their partner is "used to them," "addicted to them," "can't do without them," or "can't get anyone better." We often stay in abusive relationships because we believe that we don't deserve any better or won't get anyone better. There is a fear of loneliness or a false sense of being in the cocoon of a relationship.

Break free from such self-limiting and unhealthy thought patterns. Of course, you deserve better in life or will find someone who treats you with respect and dignity. To keep you in your place, manipulators will resort to plenty of name calling. If you express a desire, they will make you feel like you are arrogant, selfish, proud, cold, and inhumane and many other uncharitable labels.

They want to keep you dependent on them. By seeking out new opportunities for jobs, relationships, hobbies etc., you are only weakening their control over you. Seek out new people, make new friends, join a hobby club, volunteer with a non-governmental organization. Do something purposeful and meaningful that gives you the opportunity to meet new people and live a more intentional life. This is the only way to start becoming self-sufficient and independent.

9. Don't be a baby. If you are fooled once or twice, you are vulnerable, but if you constantly let people walk all over you without learning your lessons, you are a downright idiot. Stop letting manipulators take advantage of your gullibility. Develop self-awareness about manipulators and know how they operate. Have enough self-respect to refuse manipulators.

I know a lot of people who sleep walk through life, allow people to take advantage of them and then blame others for their situation. You can't go around oblivious to manipulators who are trying to use you to fulfill their agenda. Rather than blaming the evil around you, become smart and take control of your life. Yes, the unfortunate truth about life is that negative and manipulative people exist. They take advantage of people to further their agenda.

However, this shouldn't be your ticket to making the same mistakes again and again and crying foul. Manipulators cannot manipulate without the permission of their victims. Accept responsibility for your success and failure. If you are outsmarted or out strategized, it isn't someone else's fault. Learn from past mistakes. Watch out for a pattern that may reveal your own vulnerabilities. Don't keep trusting the wrong people again and again.

Similarly, don't keep giving a chronically manipulative person multiple chances. Break free from them. Remove manipulators from your life. Commit to the pursuit of surrounding yourself with positive, encouraging and like-minded folks who don't take advantage of you.

Remember, you have complete control over your life. Place your bets on yourself and not on other people. If you place your bets on other people or rely excessively on other people for your happiness, you make yourself more vulnerable to manipulation.

Again, manipulation victims are not very confident about their judgments. Learn to trust your judgments and instincts. You know what is good for you much better than anyone else. Don't go around asking people things such as, "What am I good at?" "Who is the real me?" etc. You are simply opening the doors of manipulation. Don't go around demonstrating your lack of understanding about yourself.

Again, I know a lot of people who go around seeking constant validation from others. They look at other people to define them. These people won't even buy a pair of trousers if it isn't approved by others. Why should others define you?

Define yourself and trust your judgment. Winners are not people who have a more evolved ability to listen to others. They are the ones who have developed the ability to tune in to their beliefs and judgments. They don't rely on external validation or approval of their beliefs. An established trust in your beliefs and judgments makes manipulators powerless. When you don't seek validation from others, they don't have an upper hand in how they make you think and feel. Start trusting your instinct and judgment!

10. Dependent manipulators. This is a little opposed to the stereotypical image of a manipulator, but they exist. Contrary to most manipulators, a dependent manipulator will constantly make you feel like they are powerless and completely dependent on you. They accord you the higher position in a relationship to such an extent that you feel emotionally exhausted while dealing with them.

The way to handle this type of manipulation is to gradually get them to make decisions. Make them realize that they are as much responsible for their well-being as you are. Consciously put them into positions where they are forced to make a decision. Talk to them about how their lack of responsibility to decision making is stressful for you. Over time, they may enjoy taking responsibility.

CHAPTER SEVEN

SOLID TIPS FOR INCREASING YOUR SELF-ESTEEM

The core of being manipulated is experiencing feelings of incompetency and unworthiness. Rarely will you see confident people with high self-esteem and a high sense of self-worth being manipulated. Psychological manipulators thrive on making people feel unworthy and imbalanced. By inducing this feeling of insufficiency in their victims, they attempt to gain greater power and control over the victims and, in turn, use their sense of powerlessness to fulfill selfish agendas.

One of the best ways to immunize yourself from manipulation is to develop high self-esteem and self-confidence. By having a high sense of self-worth and a positive opinion about yourself, you are preventing hungry manipulators from sabotaging you.

Here are some powerful tips for increasing your overall self-esteem to make you less susceptible to manipulation:

1. **Hold your inner critic.** Yes, we all have that niggling inner frenemy who doesn't fail to remind us of how incapable we are at doing something or how miserable our life is compared to others. This inner voice shapes your thoughts and opinions about yourself.

   Minimize your negative voice and consciously replace it with more positive and constructive terms. For instance, "I am so bad at this" can be replaced with, "I may not be good at this, but that shouldn't stop me from learning everything I can about it and mastering it." You've just given a positive twist to a hopeless statement. Choose to use more hopeful, positive and inspiring words while speaking to yourself.

   Stay, "Stop," loudly when you find your inner critic rearing its monstrous head. You can also resort to a physical gesture like pinching yourself slowly or biting your lips each time you find your inner critic in hyper active mode.

2. **Be more compassionate towards other people and treat them well.** One of the best ways to raise your own self-esteem is to treat other people with greater compassion. When you make others feel good about themselves, you automatically feel great about yourself. When you treat people well, you inspire them to treat you well in return.

   Practice kindness in your daily life by volunteering for a social cause (a huge self-esteem booster), hold the door for people, listen to someone vent, let people pass through your lane while driving, buy coffee or treats for random people, encourage a person who is feeling deflated and similar other gestures. These will go a long way in building your self-esteem.

3. **Try new things.** People who are constantly trying new things or reinventing themselves are almost always high on self-esteem. They are constantly challenging themselves by stepping outside their comfort zones. They try their hand at everything and appreciate various experiences, which increase feelings of competency.

   When you keep learning new things and developing your skills, you feel wonderful about yourself. You avoid falling into a rut. Keep trying a new adventure or picking up a new skill periodically. Nudge yourself to be active, passionate and productive. Set your spirit and soul into motion every now and then by taking up a hobby, picking up a new skill or reading an inspiring book.

4. **Avoid comparisons.** You are slowly destroying yourself by constantly comparing yourself or your life to others. There is no victory in this; you'll always lose! It is a trap that will only make you feel more inadequate and unworthy.

   Instead, look at where you were a few years ago and how far you've come to accomplish where you are today. Focus on your accomplishments and achievements today compared to a few years ago.

Albert Einstein famously said, "Everybody is a genius. But if you judge a fish by its ability to climb a tree, it will spend its whole life believing that it is stupid." Don't be that fish!

5. **Spend time with positive people.** Another great way to build your self-esteem is to surround yourself with people who support, encourage and inspire you. They should be people you look up to and should be able to influence you positively. It can be anyone from a professor to a mentor to a manager to a good friend.

Avoid interacting with people who focus on your flaws or try to bring you down at every available opportunity to feel superior about themselves. Look out for dream snatchers or people who laugh at your dreams or your ability to accomplish your goals. Self-esteem thrives in a positive environment in the midst of positive people. Be with people who make you feel good about yourself.

Also, be mindful of the books, websites and social media pages that you read. Let them charge your energy, not sap it. Don't read magazines that peddle unrealistic body images. Listen to podcasts that are naturally uplifting, empowering and inspiring the next time you find yourself with some free time at hand. Watch television shows that uplift your spirit.

6. **Sweat it out.** Countless studies have established a high correlation between exercise and a healthy self-esteem. Exercise leads to enhanced mental and physical health, which in turn,

reduces stress and makes you feel good. It also brings more discipline into your life, which invariably increases self-esteem.

Exercise doesn't have to be boring. You can take up something fun and interesting like dance, cycling, swimming, aerobics, kickboxing and more. Anything that helps you sweat and gives you a small sense of accomplishment at the end. Physical activity boosts the secretion of endorphins within the brain, which makes us "feel good." And we all know how feeling good can have a positive effect on our self-perception and self-esteem.

7. **Practice forgiveness.** Is there some grudge that you've been holding for a long time? It may be related to an ex-partner, a family member during your growing up years, a friend who betrayed you or even yourself. Don't hold on to feelings of bitterness. Overcome past feelings of shame, guilt and regret, since holding on to them will only suck you further into the circle of negativity.

CONCLUSION

Thank you again for getting a copy this book!

I hope it was able to help you to understand not just the ways through which people manipulate you but also powerful ways in which you can immunize yourself against manipulators.

The next step is to simply use all the powerful strategies and techniques used in the book to understand manipulative motives and to prevent people from manipulating you in relationships, at work and within your social circle.

There are plenty of practical tips, wisdom nuggets and real-life illustrations to help you gain a solid understanding of how manipulation works and how it can be fought in your everyday life.

Finally, if you found this book useful in any way, a review on Amazon is always appreciated!

www.ingramcontent.com/pod-product-compliance
Lightning Source LLC
Chambersburg PA
CBHW070035260726
48658CB00002B/635